The Isle of Wight's
Missing Chapter

The Isle of Wight's Missing Chapter

James Rayner

The Book Guild Ltd

First published in Great Britain in 2019 by
The Book Guild Ltd
9 Priory Business Park
Wistow Road, Kibworth
Leicestershire, LE8 0RX
Freephone: 0800 999 2982
www.bookguild.co.uk
Email: info@bookguild.co.uk
Twitter: @bookguild

Typeset in Adobe Garamond Pro

Printed and bound in Great Britain by CPI Group (UK) Ltd, Croydon, CR0 4YY

ISBN 978 1912575 992

British Library Cataloguing in Publication Data.
A catalogue record for this book is available from the British Library.

To Anna Heiða Pálsdóttir

Acknowledgements

Thanks to Gargie Ahmad, Suri Krishnamma, Wioletta Grzegorzewska, Mimi Khalvati, the Isle of Wight County Record Office, Carisbrooke Castle Museum, Ventnor and District Heritage Society and The Book Guild Ltd.

Contents

Introduction

The history of the Isle of Wight is often treated as a closed book. We know the important events that took place, how the Island developed over time, which important people came here and what life was like here in the past. It is almost as if everything has been discovered and there is nothing more to uncover.

Of course, it is important to remember the Island's links with King Charles I, Queen Victoria, Dickens, Tennyson and Keats. However, it is strange how you often find the same few stories of a handful of more obscure people such as the inventor of the Sam Browne belt retiring to Ryde and the founder of the Salvation Army having his honeymoon on the Island. These names are worthy of recognition but they have become so engrained that other, and perhaps more interesting, people have been lost from the official accounts of the Island's history.

Even some of the most talented Islanders who made a name for themselves in their day are pretty much unknown today. One such person is George Owen Wynne Apperley, who was born in Ventnor in 1884 and became a successful painter, exhibiting at the Royal Academy, with many of his works still held by leading galleries today. He spent much of his life in Spain where he painted some of his most well-known portraits of the local women he met, before moving to Tangier in Morocco where he would spend the rest of his life.

Another is Antwerp Edgar Pratt, who was born and raised in Ryde and made a name for himself as an explorer and naturalist, venturing to Tibet, the Amazon and uncharted parts of New Guinea at the turn of the 20th century. He brought back important specimens from his travels and discovered new species of plants and animals, some of which are still named after him today. The fact these people are never mentioned in relation to the history of the Isle of Wight shows that it needs to be looked at again if such talented Islanders as these have fallen off the radar.

Something else you soon notice is how most versions of the Island's history pretty much exclusively deal with British people. The Isle of Wight is still not particularly diverse today and so it is easy to presume that in the past it was the same or less so. You rarely see any mention of visitors or residents of the Island who were foreign or from an ethnic minority.

Some people on the Island will know the story of how the York Hotel in Ryde became the Royal York after the French Empress Eugénie turned up at the door early one morning having run away from France. A lot of people now know about Queen Victoria's Indian servant, Abdul Karim, who had his own cottage on the Osborne Estate. Others might know that Karl Marx came for a holiday, Ivan Turgenev to write and Mahatma Gandhi to give a talk to the Ventnor Vegetarian Society.

Less well known is that the former Queen of Portugal became a nun at Ryde in the early 20th century. Few know that the Island almost had a Jewish MP of Russian heritage called Sigismund Mendl, who just lost out in the 1892 election, and an MP of Greek heritage was almost elected by an even smaller margin in 1910, Constantine Scaramanga-Ralli.

There are few clues today to help discover the Island's international history. There is a Spindlers Road in St. Lawrence, named after the German businessman William Spindler who lived at Old Park and did much to improve the area in the late 19th century. In Sandown, there is a Guadeloupe Road which got its name from the Reverend Agassiz's Mexican-born British wife, Maria de Guadalupe Anna Antonia Robinson. The couple bought a property near the sea called Sandown Cottage, which they renamed Guadalupe House. When the house was demolished the buildings that replaced it were named Guadeloupe Terrace and even though they have gone too, the name has remained ever since, even if the spelling has changed. A recent addition is Francki Place in Cowes, named after the captain of the Polish destroyer *ORP Błyskawica* which defended the town during a heavy air raid in 1942. Other than that, there is little today that indicates the Island had anything other than a very British past.

However, the truth is that the Isle of Wight has an incredibly diverse history of people from all over the world who disembarked on the Island's shores to visit, to study, to work or to live. This is a history that goes back many centuries and is still being made today.

There were black or mixed-race Islanders being born as far back as the 1790s and dozens of Indian visitors venturing to the Island from the very first years of the Victorian era. At different times, the Island has been home to a former Jamaican model, a Japanese earthquake expert, a Sri Lankan cricketer and a pioneering Indian doctor. The Island was even visited by Maori chiefs, Argentinian students and the Queen of Hawaii. There are truly incredible stories of how the Isle of Wight plays a part in the lives of people well known in their own countries but unknown here.

Armenian priest and composer **Soghomon Soghomonian**, better known as Komitas, stayed at a small inn at Shanklin in 1911. He found inspiration walking on the Island's beaches and composed at least seven traditional Armenian songs during his time here, with the help of his companion, Armenian singer **Margaret Babaian**.

A Cameroonian teacher turned philosopher, **Bernard Nsokika Fonlon**, who would later become known as the Socrates of Cameroon, worked on the Island for seven weeks in 1955.

An Algerian from the indigenous Berber people of North Africa, described as the father of Berber nationalism, **Mohand Aarav Bessaoud**, spent the last years of his life on the Isle of Wight as a political refugee after being expelled from France in 1978. He was also a writer, founder of a Berber academy in France and is credited with designing the Berber flag.

Just from these examples you can see generally unknown stories from the Island's past coming to light, illustrating its role in the lives of people from all over the world.

Using targeted searches I have been able to uncover a whole new chapter in the Isle of Wight's history, bringing together information for the first time from history books, newspapers, biographies and official records, to tell this missing chapter from the Island's past. This book focuses on people of African, Caribbean and Indian origin, with a brief look at examples from the wider world, including China, Japan and Hawaii. However, this is just the start; there is still a wealth of information to discover about a side to the Island that is as yet little understood. European and white North American residents and visitors to the Isle of Wight have not been thoroughly investigated, simply because the length of this book would increase considerably and the more unusual stories of people from other ethnicities and nationalities would have become lost in the mass of information.

I hope that this book will shed a new light on the Island's past because its diverse history is something the Island can be proud of and it should be celebrated. It should also change the way the Island is thought about today and how the Island recognises the talent that lives here or just passes through. I hope it will also inspire people to look into this area further and bring forward their own stories of the Island's international side both from the past and in the present.

Black Georgians

It would be quite easy to presume that people of African origin are a relatively new phenomenon in the Isle of Wight's history but there is evidence that shows this relationship goes back centuries. Certainly by the Georgian period there were a significant number of black people living on the Isle of Wight and there were Islanders being born of black or mixed-race parentage. However, even before this time there were still infrequent interactions going back hundreds of years.

In the 16th century, we find a couple of reports about **Jacques Francis**, a West African diver from Arguin Island off the coast of modern-day Mauritania. In 1547, he was working in the sea off the Needles when he discovered a bell and two hundred blocks of tin and lead. Before this event, Francis had worked in the Solent when he and his Venetian master had been hired to help salvage the wreck of King Henry VIII's flagship, *The Mary Rose*.

Similarly, in 1571 we find a reference to two black men who were disembarked onto the Island from a privateering ship. They had been slaves on a Portuguese vessel bound for Brazil when they were intercepted by Sir Henry Compton on his ship, *The Castle of Comfort*. The event was bloody and the two black men were the only survivors from the raid; what happened to them after they arrived on the Island we don't know.

By the 17th century, it is likely there were black sailors amongst the many North African pirates who came to the waters around the Isle of Wight. Often referred to as Moors, they were a mixed group of people which, as well as including Arabs, Berbers and Bedouins, undoubtedly also included Sub-Saharan Africans.

Examples of their voyages close to the Island are not hard to find. In 1634, North African pirates captured John Dunton, an English sailor, and took him to Salé in modern-day Morocco to be sold. In 1636, his Algerian master invested in a slaving expedition and sent Dunton to act as pilot on the ship along with five Dutch men and twenty-one Moors. As their vessel drew near to the Isle of Wight, Dunton and the Dutch men overthrew the North Africans and took control of the ship, bringing it to dock on the Island where the eleven surviving Moors were arrested before being sent to trial at Winchester. Not many years later, an Algerian pirate known as Cannary was said to operate quite safely from the Isle of Wight attacking French and Dutch shipping and it is possible his crew included black North Africans too.

As these examples show, contact between people of African origin and the Isle of Wight was infrequent before the Georgian period; as divers, sailors, pirates and captured slaves they only made fleeting visits to the Island's coastline. This would soon change though, as black Georgians would start coming to the Island to visit, to work and to live, and the Island would develop a completely different relationship to people of this background.

There were a number of people of African, African American or West Indian origin who passed through the Island in the Georgian period, some just briefly like the black boxer **Bill Richmond**, who spent several weeks sparring and training on the Island in 1808. Another was **Joseph Mountain**, the black highwayman, who swam to the Island after having jumped off his ship in the Solent. Mountain certainly had a varied life and his autobiography describes what chain of events led to him arriving on an Isle of Wight beach in 1782.

He had been born in Philadelphia to a mixed-race father and a black mother who had been a slave for the first twenty-one years of her life. He had been a servant until the age of seventeen when his master agreed he could take a boat to Britain. Not long after his arrival he had befriended criminals and began life as a highway robber, even embarking on criminal excursions to Europe. At Gibraltar, he enlisted on a ship but as it reached Spithead on its way back to Britain, Mountain decided to bribe the sentry, jump into the sea and swim the three quarters of a mile to the Isle of Wight. He didn't stop for long and had soon made his way back to London.

Other black visitors to the Isle of Wight in the Georgian period stayed longer. The famous writer and abolitionist, **Olaudah Equiano**, spent around six months on the Isle of Wight after the death of King George II in 1760 led to his ship having to remain at Cowes. Equiano was a former slave, born in modern-day Nigeria, who bought his freedom and worked for many years on British ships. He is most well known for his autobiography, *The Interesting Narrative of the Life of Olaudah Equiano*, which includes a description of the months he spent on the Isle of Wight. He travelled all over the Island and found the people he met very polite. When he was walking through a field one day he came across a young black boy who ran to meet him being fascinated at seeing someone that looked like him. The boy took Equiano to his master's house where he was treated very kindly and they saw each other on frequent occasions until March 1761 when the ship was again ready to set sail.

As this encounter suggests, there were black people living and working on the Island at this time. It was fashionable in the Georgian period to have black servants and the boy Equiano met was not the only one to work on the Island.

At the turn of the 19th century, the parish priest for Brading and Yaverland, the Reverend Legh Richmond, came across a young black servant called **William**. He had been taken from Africa to Jamaica as a slave but after being set free now found himself employed by a naval family who had just moved to Bembridge. William asked his employer if he could help him to learn about Christianity and Richmond's ensuing interaction with the servant made up the basis of one of the stories in his book *Annals of the Poor*.

Details of another black servant on the Isle of Wight come from the will of a widow called Ellen Robinson, who left money and a large number of items to her black servant, **Colmira**. It seems Colmira had previously been employed by Mr Robinson but after his death continued to work for his widow at their house in St. Cross Lane, Newport.

4

Unfortunately Colmira died in 1801 and was buried at Church Litten, three years before her employer's death, meaning that by the time the will was enacted, Colmira was not alive to benefit from it.

Similarly, information about another black employee comes from the will of Maria Burns of Southampton, dated 1800, in which she left £100 to **Thomas Siras** (or Cyrus), described as her "old black servant now living in the Isle of Wight". During his time on the Island, Siras' wife, Ann, gives birth to a son, also called Thomas, in 1797, and a daughter, Elizabeth, in 1802. Being born on the Isle of Wight made his children Islanders and they were perhaps some of the earliest black or mixed-race Islanders. Far from being alone, there are records of other black Georgians being born on the Isle of Wight too.

Criminal records in Australia include the details of two black convicts who originated from the Isle of Wight. **John Goff** was a black seaman who had been born on the Island in the 1790s but had been sentenced to transportation to Australia. He gained a fearsome reputation in the penal colonies, no doubt enhanced by his appearance following the loss of all his front teeth after being shot in the mouth. Goff was eventually hanged at Sydney after causing two convict insurrections, including one on Norfolk Island where nearly a third of the convicts escaped.

Another was **Charles Hall**, who was born in Newport and had been a sailmaker, ploughman and labourer before freely emigrating to Australia where he was later convicted of burglary in Adelaide in 1842. It is hard to tell how many other black Islanders there were in the Georgian period, as official papers at the time rarely documented a person's ethnicity but if from these very limited sources we have already been able to establish the existence of four black Islanders, it is highly likely there were others too.

To put this into context, in the Georgian period, Britain was home to between ten and fifteen thousand people of African and West Indian origin. As we have already seen, employment as servants brought some of them to the Isle of Wight and besides those already mentioned, it is possible there were others working in country houses across the Island.

Another likely cause would be shipping, as there were a large number of black sailors during the Georgian period and black communities had already established in the port cities of Portsmouth and Southampton. Moreover, Cowes was one of the main customs posts for ships importing cargoes of rice or tobacco from America where they were often repacked and sent on to Europe. It is only because Cowes was this significant during the Georgian period that Equiano came to the Island and maybe John Goff and Charles Hall were following their fathers' professions in their work as seaman and sailmaker.

Depending on how integrated these black Islanders were, it is quite possible that they had Isle of Wight accents and spoke the Isle of Wight dialect. If Hall had been a ploughman on an Isle of Wight farm and made sails for local boat owners he certainly would have been mixing with other Islanders. They may have even had a white parent from the Island because documents at the time didn't distinguish between someone who was mixed-race and someone who was black.

As the Victorian period approached, the relationship between the Isle of Wight and people of African and West Indian origin would change again; there would still be black and mixed-race people living on the Island but many more would come just as visitors, including some that were very well known at the time.

Black Victorians and Later

In the Victorian period, the Isle of Wight was still home to people of African and West Indian origin, including three notable mixed-race Jamaicans. From 1840 to 1854, Mottistone and Shorwell had a mixed-race rector, **Ebenezer Robertson**. Born in Kingston, Jamaica, he was descended from one black great-grandparent and came to Britain to study, first at Charterhouse School, then at Cambridge University. After fourteen years as rector, he resigned his post on the Isle of Wight in 1854 over fears he would fall into poverty and later that year he committed suicide by jumping off the Shakespeare Cliff near Dover.

Another was **Henry Sewell**, who owned Steephill Castle from 1887 to 1898. His British father, William, had gone to Jamaica to work as a bookkeeper but was forced to resign by his employer because of his relationship with a mixed-race slave, Mary McCrea. The couple initially opened a small rum shop in a village nearby but after the emancipation of the slaves in Jamaica in 1838, William and Mary bought land while it was cheap and over twenty years made themselves very rich. Their son Henry was sent to Britain where he married a British woman and lived in Wales until 1887 when he bought Steephill Castle after the previous owner, Major Hambrough, went bankrupt.

Henry Sewell lived at Steephill for eleven years but usually took his boat, *The Vale Royal*, to spend winter at his Jamaican mansion, Arcadia. He sold Steephill Castle in 1898 after mounting pressure to allow the railway to reach Ventnor through the Castle's grounds. Henry had tried to fight against the proposals in court but probably sensing the inevitable, decided to sell the Castle and move away. The newspapers reported that the buyer was the director of the new railway line.

A former Jamaican model, **Fanny Eaton**, also lived on the Isle of Wight for a short period of time. Born in St. Andrew, near Kingston, she came to Britain with her mother in the 1840s. In London, she became a model for some of the most famous artists of the Pre-Raphaelite Brotherhood, including Simeon Solomon and Dante Gabriel Rossetti. In later years she worked as a domestic cook for a Hammersmith wine merchant and his wife. In the 1901 census, Fanny can be found working at the family's house in Alexandra Road, on the outskirts of Ryde.

The Isle of Wight was also home to an Ethiopian prince called **Alemayehu** for around ten months in the 1860s. When the British took Magdala in Abyssinia, his father, Emperor Tewodros II, committed suicide and the Empress died shortly afterwards. Queen Victoria requested that the orphaned Alemayehu come to Britain and so he was put under the care of Captain Tristram Speedy and was soon living at the Captain's house at Freshwater. During his time on the Isle of Wight, Prince Alemayehu went to school, learnt to ride a horse and visited the Queen at Osborne House a number of times. He had his photograph taken by Julia Margaret Cameron at Freshwater and by Jabez Hughes in Ryde. When Captain Speedy was away, Alemayehu went to stay with some of the Captain's friends at Afton, people he would come to call "grandmamma" and "grandpapa". The Prince found it particularly hard to leave these people behind when, ten months after his arrival, he moved with the Speedys to India. He would later return to Britain but sadly died from pleurisy at Leeds in 1879 aged just eighteen.

There were still some ordinary people of African and West Indian origin living on the Isle of Wight during the Victorian and Edwardian eras too. Local newspapers from the period give brief glimpses into the lives of the Island's black residents.

In 1863, the *Isle of Wight Observer* reported on a court case involving a black man called **John Abdoe**. He had been arrested for vagrancy in St. John's Park and was well known to the local police in Ryde. A policeman had seen John going to a gentleman's house, showing a begging card and asking for money. When the servant tried to send him away, he pretended not to speak English and refused to leave. In court Abdoe explained he had no friends on the Island and couldn't return to his homeland but asked if he could leave for Portsmouth where he had business. He was detained for seven days but whether he did leave the Island after his release we don't know.

In 1905, local newspapers reported on another local black man being brought, rather unjustly, before the courts. His surname seems to have been **Nelson** and he had been summoned for causing an obstruction on Newport High Street whilst demonstrating his patented knife cleaning apparatus outside Bailey's London Bazaar. The summons was later withdrawn after other evidence came to light during the court case which showed that Nelson had not committed any offence.

The Island's newspapers also reported on the heroism of a black sailor in the events following the shipwreck of *SS Irex* off Scratchell's Bay in 1890. The wreck was secured to the cliffs by a rope carried across to the ship by a coastguard's rocket. Catching in the rigging, the line allowed those on board *SS Irex* to escape safely. After the initial rescue, a boy was still seen to be in the rigging but was saved after local coastguard James Mackin and a black sailor from the crew called **Isaac Rose** went back across the line to retrieve him. Not long later, Mackin received a medal from the Royal Humane Society for his bravery but Rose received nothing. He would have remained unacknowledged had it not been for an anonymous correspondent from Freshwater, who wrote in to the *County Press* explaining that Rose had done exactly the same as Mackin and that he should receive the same recognition. The public attention this created made the Royal Humane Society reconsider and Rose was soon awarded a medal for his part in the rescue.

The Victorian period also saw a large number of black and mixed-race visitors to the Isle of Wight. One of the largest groups of these visitors were African Americans, both as freed slaves or descendants of slaves. Many came to give talks and lectures advocating the abolition of slavery in America and to raise money to free their enslaved relatives. African American abolitionists spoke all over the Island throughout the Victorian period and included some of the most well-known speakers of their day.

One of the first to visit was **Moses Roper**, who came in 1841, giving talks at such small venues as the churches and chapels of Newbridge, Chale, Rookley, Littletown, Whitwell and Wroxall, as well as Newport, Ventnor, Sandown and Shanklin. He had been a mixed-race slave whose father was also his master. Roper received such severe whippings during his time as a slave he bore permanent scars. At his events he sold his autobiography to raise money to buy the freedom of his nine enslaved brothers and sisters back in America.

Most of the African American abolitionists who came to the Isle of Wight visited during the 1850s and 1860s. This was a result of the 1850 Fugitive Slave Act in America which meant runaway slaves could be caught and sent back to their masters even in the Northern states where they had been safe from capture before. This gave many former slaves the impetus to travel to Britain, where they toured the country giving lectures and were able to write and publish their books.

William Wells Brown gave lectures on the Isle of Wight in 1850 and again in 1853, including one event where he had an audience of four hundred people and the organisers had to turn so many away they asked him to come back again.

In 1856 and 1858, **Henry "Box" Brown** brought his Grand Panorama of African and American Slavery to

Ventnor and Ryde. He became known as Henry "Box" Brown after he escaped slavery by having himself posted in a box to Philadelphia where slavery was illegal.

In 1857, **William** and **Ellen Craft** gave talks at the Victoria Rooms in Lind Street, Ryde, where they raised money to free William's sister, who was still a slave in New Orleans. The couple were well known at the time for their ingenious escape from slavery. Ellen was the daughter of a white father and a mixed-race mother which made her particularly fair for a slave. To escape she disguised herself as a white slave holder and her husband pretended to be her servant. The pair travelled by train and boat until they successfully reached the North undetected.

Other speakers to visit at the time included **John Brown**, previously known as Fed, who spoke at Ryde in 1855, **J. A. Jackson**, known for having escaped to freedom on a pony, who spoke at Newport in 1861, and the **Rev. W. M. Mitchell**, a black minister from Canada, who came to the Island in 1862.

In 1865, slavery was abolished in America which meant there was less reason for African Americans to come to the Isle of Wight to give talks, although a few still did. Later lecturers included **Josiah Henson**, who gave a talk at Ryde Town Hall in 1876 at the age of eighty-eight. He was said to be the inspiration for Harriet Beecher Stowe's book *Uncle Tom's Cabin*. In 1894, the **Rev. Thomas L. Johnson**, who had been a slave for twenty-eight years, gave a talk in Ryde on how the slaves used to escape to Canada.

Other African Americans came to the Isle of Wight in choirs, holding events to raise money. The most famous of these was the **Fisk Jubilee Singers**. They came to Ryde in 1875 when the *Isle of Wight Observer* commented on how large the audience was that came to see these singers compared to the array of empty seats there had been the night before when singers from London were performing. They were a group of former slave students, who performed to raise money for Fisk University in Nashville where they studied. They returned to the Island in 1876, performing in a marquee at Newport, and again in 1898 when they performed at the Pavilion on Ryde Pier. Another similar group were the **Canadian Jubilee Singers**, who were mainly the children of slaves who had run away to Canada to escape slavery. They came to the Island in 1883 and other groups from Georgia and Louisiana performed on the Island in 1888, 1891 and 1901.

The arts also brought other African Americans to the Isle of Wight during the Victorian period. **Ira Aldridge**, the African American actor from New York, performed at Ryde Theatre in 1860. He became well known in Britain as a Shakespearean actor and he played Othello on his first night on the Island. The mixed-race African American artist **Robert S. Duncanson** came to the Island following an invitation from Tennyson to visit him at his Freshwater home. Duncanson had painted a picture based on Tennyson's poem *The Lotus Eaters* and Tennyson asked the artist to bring the painting with him.

It is important to remember that the Isle of Wight had links to the slave trade and slave ownership, however, it is heartening to see how well received these African American visitors were to the Island. It also comes as a slight consolation to think that some of the money raised at these lectures and performances on the Island may have helped buy the freedom of some people who were still being held as slaves in America.

Aside from African Americans, the Isle of Wight also received a number of black British visitors during the Victorian era. One of the earliest was a man who went by the stage name of **Pablo Fanque**. His real name was William Darby and he had been born in Norwich, however, other details about his early life are generally uncertain. He is credited with being the first non-white circus owner in Britain and he performed to large audiences at Ryde in 1840.

Another was **Samuel Coleridge-Taylor**, a mixed-race British composer and conductor (named after the poet Samuel Taylor-Coleridge) who spent his honeymoon on the Isle of Wight. He was the son of a doctor from Sierra Leone and is best known for his three-part composition *The Song of Hiawatha* based on the work of Henry Wadsworth Longfellow. He married a white British woman on the 30th December 1899 and the couple spent the next two weeks at Shanklin where Coleridge-Taylor continued to work, arranging the music for *Hiawatha's Departure*, part of the trilogy that formed his most famous work.

It is also possible that Queen Victoria's black goddaughter came to the Island. Many people now know the story of Sara Forbes Bonetta, who was a Nigerian slave rescued from sacrifice by Captain Forbes and brought to Britain in his ship, *HMS Bonetta*. She was very close to the Queen and it is quite possible she visited Osborne House.

Her daughter, **Victoria Davies**, on the other hand,

definitely came to the Queen's Island home. She was the first child Sara had with her husband, James Pinson Labulo Davies, a wealthy businessman from Lagos in Nigeria. One source says that young Victoria Davies was staying at Sandown when Queen Victoria sent for her after having heard that the girl's mother was dying in Madeira. By the time Victoria Davies had arrived at Osborne House news had already reached them of Sara's death. When the Queen was told of the news she was said to be very upset and decided to give Victoria Davies an annuity, not only because she had lost her mother but her father's business had failed too.

The Isle of Wight also received a number of notable black South African visitors who all came to be seen by Queen Victoria. The most well known, **King Cetshwayo of the Zulus**, came in 1882. He held an important and successful talk with the Queen, which in part contributed to his return to his homeland and reinstatement as King of the Zulus.

The Queen also gave an audience to **Captain Veldtman Bikitsha** and his interpreter, **Theodore Ndwandwa**, at Osborne in 1891. Bikitsha was a leader of the Fengu people and commanded local forces allied to the British army in South Africa. He was known for his loyalty and bravery; on one occasion he was said to have killed an injured lion with his bare hands. During the meeting, the Queen presented the Captain with a walking stick and he gave her a shield and spears from his homeland.

Around the same time, the **African Choir**, a group of black South African singers, performed for Queen Victoria at Osborne House. For half of their performance they wore Western clothes and sang in English but for the other half they sang folksongs and wore their traditional clothing. There are a set of incredibly impressive photographs taken of these performers wearing clothes made from cow hide and other animal skins. As if these performers hadn't created enough interest themselves, their audience at Osborne House was said to include ladies in silk gowns, Indian servants and a West African boy in a scarlet tunic.

These visits weren't the only link between the Isle of Wight and black South Africans, as one of the most tragic and momentous incidents in South African history took place just a few miles off the Isle of Wight in 1917. The troopship **SS Mendi** was carrying a contingent of the South African Native Labour Corps (SANLC) on their way to serve on the battlefields of France when in thick fog it was struck by another boat off St. Catherine's Point and sank. Six hundred and seven black South Africans were killed in the incident and their bodies were washed up as far away as Holland and France.

Later, by the 1920s and 1930s, the Isle of Wight still received black visitors, though not in the numbers seen before. Names from this period include singer and civil rights activist **Paul Robeson**, physician **Dr John Alcindor**, singer and composer **Roland Hayes**, pianist **Lawrence Brown** and the Jamaican drug dealer and jazz musician **Eddie Manning**, whose time on the Island was spent locked in Parkhurst Prison until his death in 1931.

However, one visitor from this period that stands out from the rest is the Emperor of Ethiopia, **Haile Selassie**, who made a brief visit to Ventnor in 1938. He arrived by train with his assistant and stayed at the Beach Hotel on the Esplanade. The visit was said to be for health reasons and the Emperor tried to keep a low profile, although he was spotted by local people strolling along the promenade at dusk, wearing a cloth cap. During his stay, a local boat owner took him for a trip by sea to Puckaster Cove and the Emperor also had tea with the Irish author Henry de Vere Stacpoole in Bonchurch.

This is where we leave the story of the Isle of Wight's black Georgian, Victorian and Edwardian visitors and residents. Of course, people of African, Caribbean and African American origin have continued to come to the Island, including some very famous visitors such as musicians Jimi Hendrix, Miles Davies and Stevie Wonder. Others continue to come and make it their home and the Island maintains a small African and Caribbean minority.

What has been uncovered shows that although the Isle of Wight probably never had much of a black community in the past two hundred and fifty years, there were certainly a good number of individuals who were born here or made it their home. On top of this there were numerous black visitors, including the many anti-slavery speakers, so it would not be unreasonable to suggest that at least some Islanders would have become accustomed to interacting with people of African or West Indian origin on the Isle of Wight.

It is important to remember that the Isle of Wight did have links with the slave trade and slavery, however, it is also important to remember how well received anti-slavery speakers were when they came to give talks on the Island. The Isle of Wight also certainly played an important part in black history as the location of a meeting which led to

Cetshwayo being restored as King of the Zulus, as well as being the site of the disastrous sinking of the *SS Mendi*. Of course, the individuals we have covered do not provide an exhaustive list of everyone of this background who made it to the Isle of Wight and no doubt there are still many more to discover.

Indian Residents

Until relatively recently, it seems that there weren't significant numbers of Indian residents on the Isle of Wight but there were a handful of individuals living here at different times since the last decades of the Victorian era. One group of temporary residents who came and went throughout the year were the Indian servants who lived and worked at Osborne House when the Queen was on the Island.

Most people now know the story of Queen Victoria and her Indian servant, **Abdul Karim**, who had his own cottage on the Osborne estate. He was known by the title *Munshi*, as he taught the Queen the Urdu language. She even learnt phrases such as "The tea is always bad at Osborne". In later years his family were allowed to come over from India and live on the estate with him. It is a good thing that Abdul Karim is now recognised, however, he was not the only Indian servant that lived and worked at Osborne House.

In the corridor that leads to the Durbar Room are a large number of portraits of Indian sitters. Many of these were pictures of the Queen's Indian subjects, living in India, but mixed in amongst these paintings are several depicting the Queen's Indian servants who worked for the Royal Household. The earliest of these paintings are of Abdul Karim, **Mohammed Bukhsh** and **Sheikh Saiyad Ahmad Hussain**, who were all painted at Osborne by the Austrian painter Rudolf Swoboda in the summer of 1888.

Bukhsh accompanied Abdul when he first arrived in Britain but was soon outshone by him, as he was older and considered less attractive. The most well-known photograph of Abdul Karim and Mohammed Bukhsh was actually taken by the photographers Hughes and Mullins of Ryde. Sheikh Saiyad Ahmad Hussain was another of the first Indian servants who worked for the Queen but he too was sidelined at the expense of Karim, which made him unhappy and depressed.

From photographs and descriptions in the local newspapers of the Royal Family's *tableaux vivants* (scenes created with motionless, silent actors) we can prove other Indian servants also came to the Island when the Queen did, including **Mirza Yusuf Beg** and **Ahmad Khan**. Documents also prove that the cooks **Ghulam Mustafa** and **Sheikh Chidda** both worked on the Island and they may have made the chicken curry which was a regular feature on the menu at Osborne at the Queen's request.

It is also because of Queen Victoria that another Indian came to live briefly on the Isle of Wight. The Punjabi architect **Bhai Ram Singh** was brought over from Lahore to design the carvings and wooden plaster moulds for the Durbar Room at Osborne House. He was given his own cottage to stay in while he supervised the work. The Queen met him on site in January 1891 to be shown his plans and sketches. She later described him as a very intelligent and pleasant man. Bhai Ram Singh spent Christmas that year at Osborne and as a present Queen Victoria gave him a signed portrait and a gold pencil case. When the work was completed in 1892, Rudolf Swoboda was commissioned to paint Bhai Ram Singh, creating another of the portraits that still hangs at Osborne House today.

Beyond the grounds of Osborne though, there were never many Indians living on the Isle of Wight during the Victorian era. Census records give us a few examples, such as the Indian servant working for a captain of an East Indian cavalry regiment at his house in Ryde in 1851 and an Indian student who was staying at a boarding house in Shanklin in 1901. Though not many in number, amongst them were two people from the Indian subcontinent who made a name for themselves, both starting their careers in Britain on the Isle of Wight at around the same time.

The first was an Indian doctor called **David J. A. Chowry-Muthu**, who had come to Britain to study medicine. Dr Chowry-Muthu's first contact with the Isle of Wight was in 1899 when he used to come down from London every week to supervise at Mount Pleasant Sanatorium, a medical facility for treating tuberculosis, in Dudley Road, Ventnor. By 1901 he was living on the Island at his own larger sanatorium called Inglewood, located in St. Lawrence. His family came to the Island with him and lived in the lodge next door, his son Philip Leslie Muthu being born on the Island in the same year.

It was during his time here that Dr Chowry-Muthu started trialling a new method of treating tuberculosis. He used formaldehyde which was inhaled as a gas and used in conjunction with the open-air method of treatment; at the time there had only been very limited trials. He had patients come to Inglewood for treatment from all over Britain and by 1902 he was writing to the *British Medical Journal* about his results treating one hundred patients with this method. He wrote a number of other articles for medical journals during his time on the Island which illustrate his contributions to medical research, including one suggesting that even if there is no tuberculosis bacteria found in a patient's saliva, the disease may still be present in their lungs.

At some point in 1902, Dr Chowry-Muthu moved to a new sanatorium in Somerset but this wouldn't be the end of his connection to the Island, as he would return in later years during his retirement.

Another notable Isle of Wight resident from the Indian subcontinent arrived around the same time as Dr Chowry-Muthu. Known as Ranji, **Alfred Holsinger** was born in Colombo in Sri Lanka and came to Britain in 1899 to pursue his passion for cricket. He gained fame as the first professional cricketer from an ethnic minority to play in the English Leagues.

The first club he played for in 1899 was Ryde, where he took a wicket with the first ball he bowled on British soil. In 1901, he married a woman from the Island, Elizabeth Adeline Poiney. She had been living with her mother, who was a lodging-house keeper in Green Street, and if Holsinger had stayed there on his arrival at Ryde it is possible that is how the pair met each other.

After their marriage the couple moved to Weeks Road and their first child was born in the same year. In 1905, the death of their second child at just a few months old made the local newspapers because of the unusual nature of the child's death. He had been found unresponsive, hanging over the edge of the basket he slept in, and couldn't be revived by the doctor. It was concluded that the child had suffered a fit and he was later buried at Ryde Cemetery. By 1906, the family had moved to Dewsbury in Yorkshire and Alfred Holsinger would go on to play cricket in Lancashire and Lincolnshire.

As you can see, whilst there were not many Indian residents on the Isle of Wight during the Victorian and Edwardian eras, it is safe to say that those who lived here were no ordinary people. Especially Dr Chowry-Muthu using pioneering medical techniques and Alfred Holsinger starting his international cricketing career at Ryde; these are definitely achievements the Island should be proud of. However, despite the small number of Indian residents, the Isle of Wight was certainly no stranger to Asian people as we are about to see as we take a look at some of the multitude of Indian visitors who came to the Island in the 19th and early 20th centuries.

Abolitionist and author Olaudah Equiano who spent six months
on the Isle of Wight in the 1760s

(British Library)

The African American actor Ira Aldridge dressed as Othello, the
character he played on his first night at Ryde Theatre

(National Library of Poland)

JABEZ HUGHES   RYDE. I.W.

Prince Alemayehu of Abyssinia who stayed at Freshwater and
Afton during his ten months on the Island

(©National Portrait Gallery)

Emperor Haile Selassie of Ethiopia, with his assistant,
disembarking on Ventnor Beach in 1938

(Ventnor and District Local History Society)

The Maharajah Duleep Singh who first
visited Osborne House in 1854

The Princess of Coorg who was a frequent visitor to Ryde in the
middle of the 19th century

(Slovak National Gallery)

Zhan Shichai, also known as the Chinese Giant, who came to Ryde in the winter of 1890

The Japanese earthquake specialist Shinobu Hirota who lived at
Shide Hill House near Newport

The Isle of Wight-born writer and film director Suri Krishnamma

The Iranian poet Mimi Khalvati who studied at Upper Chine School in Shanklin from the age of six until sixteen

(© Caroline Forbes, via Mimi Khalvati)

Wioletta Grzegorzewska, a Polish author and Man Booker Prize nominee who lived in Ryde for ten years

(Wioletta Grzegorzewska)

Indian Visitors

Indian visitors to the Isle of Wight started arriving during the very first years of the Victorian period and continued to arrive steadily until at least the 1930s. They came from a wide range of backgrounds and travelled here for a number of different reasons. Amongst them were writers, sailors, revolutionaries, servants, holy men and even Indian royalty.

One of the first to visit was **Mohan Lal Zutshi**, a Kashmiri spy who had worked for the British in Afghanistan and is credited with assassinating the Afghan Resistance leader, Mir Masjidi Khan. When he made a tour of Britain in 1844, his first stop was the Isle of Wight having been invited by Sir Claude Wade, who Mohan Lal had worked with in India. Wade was now living at Brigstocke Terrace in Ryde, where he had relocated to following his retirement from service in India.

Mohan Lal was only on the Island for a few days but visited every part, travelling for up to fourteen hours each day. He was even spotted at Ventnor by the British author George Mogridge, who later wrote about Lal's gold embroidered jacket, green slippers and velvet cap. Lal was impressed by the Island's natural beauties and swam in the sea every day, writing that he felt "refreshed to a degree quite impossible to express". Sir Claude introduced him to many of his friends on the Island and Mohan Lal found he was having breakfast, lunch and dinner each at different venues.

Lal had studied in India with **Mir Shahamet Ali**, who also came to the Island a few years later. Ali rented a cottage in Ryde and finished his book *Notes and Opinions of a Native on the Present State of India and the Feelings of Its Peoples*. He had it published in Ryde in 1848 by local printer George Butler, who worked out of the Colonnade in Lind Street. Butler was also the publisher of local newspaper the *Isle of Wight Observer* and his wife carried on the business for years after George's death.

During his time on the Island, Shahamet Ali invited his Lebanese friend Habib Risk-Allah Effendi to spend a few days with him. In fact this visit lasted over a month and Risk-Allah was also introduced to Sir Claude and other important residents of Ryde. The two men eventually left the Island together, Ali heading for Mecca feeling the need to purify himself after mixing so much with Christians and Risk-Allah accompanying him as far as Paris.

Not many years later would be the **Maharajah Duleep Singh**'s first visit to Osborne House. He was the last Maharajah of the Sikh Empire, who was deposed when the British annexed the Punjab. In 1854, aged just fifteen, the Maharajah was invited by Queen Victoria to visit her Island home. The Queen and Singh made sketches of each other and he gave the princes Indian costumes he had brought with him. They developed a strong and lasting connection;

Duleep Singh was often invited to Osborne and the Queen became godmother to his children. It seems his family sometimes came to the Island as well. Newspaper reports suggest two of the Maharajah's daughters were staying at Totland in 1891 and there are photographs of his part-German, part-Ethiopian wife from Egypt, Bamba Müller, and his first son, Victor Albert Singh, which were both taken by photographers in Ryde.

Other Indian visitors also came following invitations from Queen Victoria, including the Bengali Hindu philosopher and social reformer, **Keshub Chandra Sen**. Sen came to Osborne in August 1870 where he was served a vegetarian lunch before being taken to see the Queen and Princess Louise. The Queen presented Sen with signed copies of her two books, *Early Years of the Prince Consort* and *Highland Journal*. In return he gave her two portraits of his wife, Jaganmohini, which the Queen was so pleased with that she requested a portrait of him too.

The Maharajah Duleep Singh was not the only member of Indian royalty to come to the Isle of Wight either. The deposed **Princess of Coorg** was known to be a frequent visitor. After the British took control of the Kingdom of Coorg in Southern India, the princess and her father, the former Rajah, travelled to Britain. Queen Victoria took care of the princess, whose father's health was deteriorating, and she was baptised Victoria Gouramma at Buckingham Palace in 1852. She was looked after by a number of different people, including Lady Harcourt who Gouramma often came to stay with at her home, St. Clare's, located in Appley on the outskirts of Ryde. Reports state the princess came to the Island for her health and show she was here for a couple of summers in the 1850s and possibly during the 1860s as well.

Not long after Queen Victoria's death in 1901, the Maharani of the princely state of Cooch Behar stayed at Osborne Cottage as the guest of Princess Beatrice, who was Royal Governor of the Island at the time. The Maharani's name was **Suniti Devi** and she was the daughter of Keshub Chandra Sen, who had visited Queen Victoria in 1870. Another royal was **Ripudaman Singh**, who was the next in line to become the Maharajah of the princely state of Nabha when he, his family and his Indian servants stayed at Melbourne House in Ventnor in 1911. Just months later his father died and he succeeded to the title of Maharajah. A fleeting visit was also made by the **Maharajah of Burdwan**, who came to East Cowes for the day in 1906 to see the Royal Naval College at Osborne.

Other Indian visitors came to the Island for a variety of different reasons. The most famous of these was **Mahatma Gandhi**, although he was not well known at the time of his visit. Still a law student in 1891, he visited the Island to give a talk to the Ventnor Vegetarian Society. He was accompanied by the lawyer **Tryambakrai Mazmudar** who Gandhi had sailed with from India. The speech did not go well; Gandhi described how his vision became blurred and he trembled; in the end Mazmudar had to read it for him. Gandhi was staying with a vegetarian family in Ventnor and the daughter of the landlady took Gandhi for a walk up the hills around the town but he struggled to keep up with her and found the experience a bit humiliating.

Maulvi Rafiuddin Ahmad was a barrister, journalist and politician, who also stayed at Ventnor when he came to the Island to visit Tennyson in 1892. At the poet's Freshwater home, Ahmad was surprised and impressed to see how many books of translated Persian literature Tennyson had on his shelves.

Religious visitors include **Sadhu Singh**, an Indian Christian missionary, who made a low-profile trip to the Island in the 1920s. He was incredibly shy and the only exercise he took during his stay was by walking up and down the roof terrace of the house he was staying in.

Visiting writers include **Ardaser Sorabjee N. Wadia**, who spent a few days here in 1917, where he seemed to delight in trespassing on various lawns. Finding a side-gate open at the Royal Yacht Squadron, at the time one of the most exclusive clubs in the world, Wadia made a quick circuit of their lawn and later at Farringford, ignoring the sign against trespassing, he climbed over a gate because he said he couldn't resist walking amongst the daffodils.

The philosopher and speaker **Jiddu Krishnamurti** stayed at Shanklin in 1914 when he was still a child on a studying holiday with his tutors. During his time here he also learnt to play golf and it was in the woods around the town that he apparently first began to see mythical creatures.

Some Indian revolutionaries briefly passed through the Island during this period too. **K. V. R. Swami**, who was under observation by the government, came here for medical treatment in 1910, and **Udham Singh**, who would later assassinate the former Lieutenant Governor of the Punjab, entered Britain on a fake passport in 1933 and stayed with an IRA leader on the Island.

Waris Ameer Ali became an adviser on Indian matters to Sir Winston Churchill in later life but both men shared something in common from their childhoods. Churchill often came to Ventnor for his holidays as a child and Waris visited the town in 1901 at the age of fourteen. He stayed at the Marine Hotel with his British mother and his brother, **Torick Ameer Ali**. Their father, Syed, was a well-known Islamic scholar and legal expert, who was the first Muslim elected to the Privy Council.

Other names who crossed the Solent include the writer **Patras Bokhari**, historian and translator **Romesh Chunder Dutt**, the Prime Minister of Hyderabad, **Sir Salar Jung**, religious figure **Champat Rai Jain** and the Communist MP for Battersea North, **Shapurji Saklatvala**.

Aside from these well-known people from the Indian subcontinent, ordinary South Asian visitors came to the Isle of Wight too, many through working as sailors. For hundreds of years British ships employed sailors known as lascars, who usually came from the Indian subcontinent but sometimes from South East Asia as well. A report from 1906 showed that there were over 38,000 lascars working on British ships who accounted for seventeen percent of the workforce.

One of the earliest encounters between this group of people and the Isle of Wight was a tragic event which took place at the end of the 18th century. Around the same time that the *HMS Royal George* sank off Ryde, an East Indiaman ship with a lascar crew sailed to Spithead. Ravaged by disease, many of the crew died and were buried on the beach at Ryde. Reports of later years mention this event when skeletons were discovered during building works on what had been Ryde Duver but which became the Esplanade and the Strand. They described how "immense" numbers of lascars were among those buried in the sand, along with Russian sailors and the victims of the *Royal George*.

Another unfortunate incident occurred when a ship called the *Duke of Westminster* ran onto rocks and became stuck fast at Atherfield Ledge in 1884. Amongst the crew who were forced to abandon the ship and come ashore were a number of lascar sailors who were almost immediately sent off to Portsmouth and London.

A number of articles give details of lascars who had committed crimes aboard their ships and were then brought to court or imprisoned on the Island. In 1918, a lascar sailor called **Abbas Ali** was brought before the judge at Newport for wounding his colleague by stabbing him in the chest following a disagreement. Another lascar sailor called **Bhagwase Jassiwarra** was found guilty of murder at a trial held in Lancaster and sent to serve his sentence at Parkhurst Prison, where he died from tuberculosis in 1898.

It also seems that some lascar sailors may have stayed on the Isle of Wight for longer periods of time. At least, there is evidence that Newport was briefly home to a South Asian sailor called **Deen Mohamed**. He is documented because in 1856 he was twice brought before the courts for assaulting Louisa Row, a woman he cohabited with. Described as a travelling lascar, he had been in Newport for some time selling perfume. After the first incident he was released on the promise that he would leave the Isle of Wight but a week later he was back in court for having assaulted Louisa again; this time he was sent to Winchester Prison.

In later years, another big draw for ordinary South Asians was the annual **Indian Social Conference**, also known as the Indian Annual Reunion. This started as a social event held every Easter for hundreds of Indian students across Britain to get together, usually involving music and sports matches played against local teams. During the 1930s, the Isle of Wight was often chosen as the destination, as was the case in the 1950s by which time the event had changed into one for the whole British Asian community from across the country to meet together with their families.

This is where we leave the Island's Asian connections behind. As you can see, there were few Indians who made the Isle of Wight their home but amongst those that did were two individuals whose work broke new ground: Dr Chowry-Muthu, who undertook pioneering tuberculosis treatments, and the Sri Lankan cricketer Alfred Holsinger, starting his international career at Ryde. Both of these men should be remembered for their achievements but also because their children were possibly some of the first Islanders to be born with Asian heritage, quite remarkable for the turn of the 20th century.

We have also seen how popular the Island was with Indian visitors, looking at a number of different examples, although there were no doubt many more. Amongst them we have found well-known individuals such as Mahatma Gandhi and Duleep Singh but also more ordinary people such as servants and sailors. Considering the high number of Indian visitors and the multitude of different reasons that brought them to the Island, it is quite possible that some Islanders would have become accustomed to interacting with people of an Asian background.

Today, the Isle of Wight's Asian connections have never been stronger. The Island is now home to a significant Asian minority, there is a mosque in Newport and in recent years events have been held to mark the Hindu festival of light, Diwali. Asian visitors continue to come, including DJ and radio presenter Nihal Arthanayake who has performed at both the Bestival and the Isle of Wight Festival, and an Asian film crew who used the Island as a location in 2017. Osborne House is now part of the Anglo Sikh Heritage Trail and the Island as a whole remains a popular holiday destination for British Asian tourists.

The Wider World

So far we have delved into the Island's connections with people of African, Caribbean and Indian origin, who were no doubt the most numerous non-white visitors and residents on the Isle of Wight during the Georgian, Victorian and Edwardian periods. People from other ethnic groups outside of Europe and America were certainly few and far between at this time but some did end up on the Island's shores, some from really remote or unusual places. These people also have interesting stories to tell of what chain of events led them here or what they did after their arrival.

One group worth examining are the Japanese residents of Shide Hill House, who lived on the Island for a number of years, amongst them one individual in particular who assisted in carrying out groundbreaking new research in the field of earthquake studies. The house they lived in, Shide Hill House, had become the home of the famous Liverpool-born geologist and earthquake expert, John Milne.

Milne had originally travelled to Japan as a foreign adviser on mining and geology but soon became involved in the study of earthquakes and co-founded the Seismological Society of Japan. He is credited with inventing the horizontal pendulum seismograph (which measures earthquakes) and was awarded the Order of the Rising Sun by the Japanese Emperor. Milne married **Tone**, daughter of Horikawa Noritsune, and after a fire in 1895 which destroyed his home, observatory and many of his instruments, he resigned his post and the couple moved to Britain.

Arriving at Shide Hill House, the pair were also accompanied by Milne's Japanese assistant seismologist, **Shinobu Hirota**. Within a week of arriving, Hirota had set up the seismograph he had brought with him from Japan and not much time later another was established at Carisbrooke Castle which Hirota looked after, walking the four miles every day from Shide to attend to it. He assisted John Milne with his work, helping him produce his "Shide Circular Reports on Earthquakes" which were published annually for twelve years. Hirota also invented an instrument which had sat in the cellars of the Royal Victoria Yacht Club at Ryde for a number of years measuring the sinking and rising of the earth caused by the weight of water in the Solent as the tide rose and fell.

But it wasn't only the study of earthquakes that Hirota undertook during his time on the Island. During the early 1900s, he was also an active member of the Isle of Wight Photographic Club which had elected Milne as its president. There are frequent reports which give reference to Hirota's activities in the club, giving demonstrations on enlarging photos, retouching and lantern-slide making. He even devised a photograph-developing competition which revealed portraits of Milne and well-known local golfers "in striking attitudes" on the green of Newport Golf Club.

In 1906, Shinobu Hirota took a trip back to Japan taking photos which were later used to illustrate a talk held by John Milne called "Chat about Japan and the Japanese". It seems that Shinobu also got married during this visit back to his homeland because after he had returned to Britain we find his wife **Masaji Hirota** also listed as living at Shide Hill House.

Aside from these three Japanese residents, there were also a number of visitors who came to see Milne on the Island, drawn by his enduring fame in Japan, including mathematician **Baron Dairoku Kikuchi**. However, things started to change in December 1912 when Shinobu Hirota returned home following the advice of his doctor, his wife accompanying him. In 1913, John Milne died and his wife, Tone, found it difficult to remain in Britain but was forced to stay for the duration of the First World War, eventually returning to Japan in 1919.

Milne was buried in St. Paul's churchyard on Staplers Road and occasionally Japanese visitors to the Island still visit his grave today. As you can see, these people were no ordinary residents, especially Shinobu Hirota who had lived on the Island for around seventeen years, carrying out his earthquake investigations as well as getting involved in a photographic sideline.

There are some particularly interesting stories surrounding a number of individuals from these other regions of the world who came to visit the Island too. The most unusual have to be the stories of the Chinese giant, who only went out at night during the few months he spent at Ryde; the

King of the Cocos Islands, who died at Ventnor and was temporarily buried at Bonchurch; and Queen Emma of Hawaii, who hid amongst Tennyson's cabbages.

In the winter of 1890, a Chinese giant came to visit the Island. Born **Zhan Shichai** in Fuzhou in South East China in the 1840s, he grew to over eight foot tall and became known as the Chinese Giant. He left China to earn a living touring as a curiosity under the stage names Chang Woo Gow and Chang Yu-Sing. He went to London in 1865 and later to Sydney in Australia where he met his future wife.

After giving up touring he settled in Bournemouth where he opened a Chinese tea house with his wife. His health became worse in later years, which brought Zhan to Ryde in 1890 where he was under the supervision of a local doctor, Dr Johnston. Zhan stayed at a house in Melville Street but kept a low profile because of the interest his appearance created, often only going out for a walk in the evenings. He obviously did a good job of hiding because although he spent several months at Ryde, it wasn't until he was leaving that local journalists become aware that the famous Chinese Giant had been staying in the town. By March he had returned home to Bournemouth but would come back to the Island a few months later for another brief visit.

At the turn of the century, **George Clunies-Ross** died at Ventnor and was temporarily buried at Bonchurch, until arrangements were made to return his body to his homeland. Clunies-Ross was the part-Scottish, part-Malay "King of the Cocos Islands", being the head of state for this group of coral islands located in the Indian Ocean. This unofficial title was given to him as the third generation of the Clunies-Ross family who were the original settlers of the Cocos Islands, owning most of the property and the only employer of the local people.

Uninhabited when the Clunies-Ross family arrived in 1826, they set up a coconut harvesting industry and invited Malay people to come to the islands and work for them. George's father's family originally came from Shetland but his mother, S'pia Dupong, was a Malay woman and he himself would marry one of the Malay settlers. The Cocos Islands were claimed by Great Britain and in 1886 they were granted by Queen Victoria to George Clunies-Ross and his descendants.

In 1910, George became ill and for his health came to Ventnor, where one of his married daughters was said to be living. Not long after his arrival he died. It was intended his body would be returned to the Cocos Islands for burial but his body remained several months with an undertaker in Bonchurch. It was decided to bury him at St. Boniface churchyard but this caused controversy as an objection was made that for legal reasons "strangers" were not allowed to be buried there. The rector defended his decision, saying that the man had already been in Bonchurch for three months with an undertaker and there was no other option. He only remained buried on the Island for a few years because in 1914 arrangements were finally made to take his body back to his former kingdom on the Cocos Islands.

Queen Emma of Hawaii came to the Island in 1865, accompanied by a native Hawaiian priest called William Hoapili and his wife, Kiliwehi. Queen Emma had come to the Isle of Wight specifically to see Lord

Tennyson at Farringford because of her appreciation of literature. Unfortunately, her arrival at Freshwater caused such interest on the Island that guests kept calling in to Tennyson's home hoping to be introduced to the Queen of Hawaii. The Tennysons decided to hide Queen Emma in a summer house in the kitchen garden, so she could read her letters in peace. She later described this hiding place as being "among the cabbages". The Queen was taken for a walk up the Down and Mr and Mrs Hoapili sang traditional Hawaiian songs for the Tennyson family. She seemed to enjoy her time at Farringford but she had a busy few days on the Island trying to raise money to build a cathedral in Hawaii. She attended an event in the Orangery of Steephill Castle and made a brief appearance at Ryde Town Hall.

It is not hard to find examples that illustrate how visitors to the Island came from every corner of the world. Queen Victoria alone received all sorts of different people at Osborne House, such as the group of thirteen Maori chiefs and three Maori women who came in 1863, some of the men wearing capes of pigeon, kaka parrot and kiwi feathers. Other guests who visited the Queen on official business include **King Rama V of Siam**, **Dom Pedro II of Brazil, Francisco Solano López of Paraguay** and diplomatic representatives from Burma, Morocco, Zanzibar, Abyssinia and the Ottoman Empire.

Other illustrious people who came to different parts of the Island include the exiled Mexican Emperor, **Agustín de Iturbide**. He set sail from the Isle of Wight in 1824 on his way back to Mexico after his supporters encouraged him to return. However, not long after he had disembarked at Soto la Marina to an enthusiastic welcome, he was arrested and later executed by firing squad.

Mai, the first Pacific Islander to come to Britain in the 1770s, visited the Isle of Wight during his two-year stay. Also known as Omai, he came from the Society Islands, now part of French Polynesia, travelling to Britain on *HMS Adventure.* He spent most of his time in London, where he met Dr Samuel Johnson, but in the company of naturalist Joseph Banks also visited a number of places on the South Coast. Whilst on the Island they took an excursion to the cliffs near the Needles to shoot sea birds, a common sport for tourists during this time.

The Chilean painter **Pedro Subercaseaux** was for many years a monk at Quarr Abbey in the 1920s and 1930s, eventually leaving to set up a new monastery in Santiago.

In the middle of the 20th century there were even a number of important Tibetans who made their way here. In 1960, the Dalai Lama's mother, **Dekyi Tsering**, stayed at Freshwater for six weeks to recover from an operation, and the Tibetan doctor and author **Tsewang Y. Pemba** described how in his youth he had visited Quarr Abbey.

There were ordinary people too who you find occasional mention of in the local newspapers, including the Algerian carpet seller, **Slemane Ben Durred**, who had an altercation with a local man in Ventnor in 1906. Another was the Japanese sailor **Tetsunosuke Suzuki**, who died on board the Japanese ship *Fuji* which was anchored in the Solent in 1897. He was buried at Ryde and even five years later when other Japanese ships were in the area, groups of Japanese sailors disembarked and marched in formation to Ryde Cemetery to visit the sailor's grave.

Although there is literally a world of other stories still to tell we have established a start, illustrating how the Isle of Wight has a great international past which has until now generally been kept hidden.

So far, the image of the Island's international history we have created has only been brought together from freely available and easily accessible sources. There are so many areas which would uncover much more of this history if they were investigated further. For example, the Island received large numbers of international students who came during the 19th and early 20th centuries, studying at various official and unofficial schools.

Appuldurcombe House was once an educational institution and amongst the students there in 1891 we find two Middle Eastern children named Hayder and Alexander Keun. Their father was from a Dutch family but born in Smyrna (now Izmir in Turkey) and worked as a Dutch diplomat in the Middle East. His wife was an Arab from Baghdad (in Iraq) and that is where Hayder was born. Alexander, also known as Iskender, had been born later in Bushehr (in Iran) where the boys' father worked as Consul-General.

Other examples include the four native Hawaiian girls who were sent to study at a short-lived Foreign Mission school established at Blackgang. Another can be found in the 1901 census which records five Argentinian students living in Arreton, three at the vicarage where they were taught and two others staying with local people in nearby houses. It would be really interesting to investigate the Island's international students further and find out if any of them went on to achieve great things or become well known.

To create this history, evidence and information have come from a multitude of different sources including obscure and unlikely places. Not all information about the Isle of Wight comes from obvious sources and sometimes evidence which sheds new light on the subject is found in the most unassuming of documents.

To illustrate this point, you can find a reference to the Isle of Wight in the autobiography of the Pakistani author and human rights campaigner Tehmina Durrani, which mainly revolves around her volatile relationship with her husband during the 1970s. In this book she mentions that her sister Minoo, whilst rebelling against her parents, insisted she was going to the Isle of Wight to study photography. Her parents at first resisted but after seeing how determined their daughter was they relented and rented a flat on the Island for her to live in while she enrolled at the photographers' school.

Similarly, it was only by searching a number of keywords together that a reference to the Island came to light in a biography of the man described as "The Socrates of Cameroon", teacher turned philosopher Bernard Nsokika Fonlon, who worked on the Island for seven weeks in 1955. There is, no doubt, a multitude of fascinating references to the Island still to uncover from all sorts of different sources but that is an exciting prospect yet to be fully explored.

Although the focus of this book has been on people of African, Caribbean and Indian origin, these examples show how the people who came to the Island to visit or to live really did come from every corner of the world. This work hasn't even touched on the multitude of Europeans or white Americans who came, because if it had done the book would be three or four times as long. This is another area that still needs to be looked into and I'm sure the Island's past will have a few surprises here too.

A New Image of the Island

Looking back over what has just been uncovered we see an Island which, in the Georgian, Victorian and Edwardian periods, experienced great diversity in its residents and visitors. There is still so much yet to uncover in this chapter of the Isle of Wight's history but already we have found such vibrancy and interest. This has to create a re-evaluation of the Island's past because it challenges the way it has been thought about up until now.

Sometimes when people talk about islands in general, they use the word "insular" in the sense of being inward-looking and perhaps narrow-minded, or the phrase "Island mentality" referring to isolation and its perceived effects. However, even if some people consider this appropriate to apply to the Isle of Wight today, do these labels have any justification in the Island's past? Considering the global nature of the stories that make up the Island's history, there is a lot to indicate that many people on the Isle of Wight were actually very tolerant and accepting of different nationalities and ethnicities as far back as the Georgian period.

We have found that there were mixed marriages on the Island over a hundred years ago. Alfred Holsinger, Dr

Chowry-Muthu and Henry Sewell all had British wives and the black Islanders who were born here as early as the 1790s could have been the children of mixed marriages as well because the records don't specify. Then to have Islanders born in the late 18th century with African or West Indian parentage and other Islanders born in the first years of the 20th century with Asian heritage indicates a remarkable level of inclusiveness.

Also, think of the hospitality and interest that Islanders showed to the visitors who came here and residents that lived here, the kindness that Equiano and Zutshi wrote about. Think of the more than four hundred people that turned out to see William Wells Brown speak against slavery in Newport and the correspondent from Freshwater making sure the black sailor Isaac Rose got the recognition he deserved. Imagine the locals of Shorwell and Mottistone in 1840 listening to their church service delivered by their mixed-race vicar who perhaps still had a Jamaican accent. Consider the nearly 48% of Islanders voting for a Jewish candidate to represent them at Parliament in 1892 and the widow from Newport leaving in her will a substantial amount of money and possessions to her black servant Colmira.

Even amongst the British Islanders there is a sense of an outward-looking perspective. When we rediscover people such as Antwerp Edgar Pratt, who went from Ryde to the Amazon, Tibet and uncharted parts of New Guinea, and George Owen Wynne Apperley who, after a life in Europe painting portraits of Spanish gypsies, lived the last of his days at Tangier in Morocco. Facts like this just show that the Isle of Wight's history definitely needs to be reconsidered because these discoveries challenge what we thought we knew about the Island.

But this story is not just set in the past. There are people alive now with international backgrounds but Isle of Wight connections who are continuing to create this diverse story.

One family who have arguably served as some of the best ambassadors for the Island are the Minghella family, who originate from Italy. The late **Anthony Minghella**, who passed away in 2008, was an Oscar-winning film director, playwright and screenwriter, most famous for his films *The English Patient* (1996) and *The Talented Mr Ripley* (1999). His brother **Dominic Minghella** is a well-known television producer and screenwriter. Anthony and Dominic were both born on the Island and their parents are also influential for having created one of the Isle of Wight's most famous exports, Minghella Ice Cream.

Similarly, the Iranian poet, actress and theatre director **Mimi Khalvati** has served the Island as an unofficial ambassador by immortalising it in her works. Though born in Tehran, from the age of six until sixteen she was a boarder at Upper Chine School in Shanklin. Growing up here created such an impression on her that many years later when she published *The Chine* you find the landscape and buildings of the Isle of Wight at the forefront of her poetry.

A mixed-race Islander who has made a name for himself is the film director and writer **Suri Krishnamma**. Born in Shanklin in 1961 to an Indian father and a British mother, he is now also Professor of Film at Norwich University of the Arts. His films have won awards and been nominated for BAFTAs; one of his very first productions, entitled *New Year's Day*, even used the Isle of Wight as the location. His brother **Ranjit Krishnamma** was also born on the Island and is now a theatre and television actor. He has performed at the Royal National Theatre and appeared in a number of well-known BBC and ITV dramas including *The Bill*, *Casualty* and *Eastenders*.

Also, the Island still maintains a Caribbean connection in the form of singer and local celebrity **Derek Sandy**, who originates from Trinidad and Tobago. He has also represented the Island in his music, with his most famous song *Welcome to the Isle of Wight* almost serving as the Island's unofficial anthem.

Another name that should be celebrated on the Isle of Wight is **Wioletta Grzegorzewska** but in fact few people on the Island know about her existence. Also known as Wioletta Greg, she is a famous Polish author who lived in Ryde for about ten years. She originally came from a village in Southern Poland but moved to the Isle of Wight in 2006. She has found the Island a source of inspiration and you see it featured in her poetry and prose. One of her poems is called *Bezsenność w Ryde* (Sleepless in Ryde) and another of her works is entitled *Notatnik z wyspy* (Notes from an Island) which gives a more day-to-day description of her life here.

Wioletta's reputation has been building recently. You can now find her works being translated into a number of languages and her audience expanding beyond Polish speakers. She has been nominated for a number of international awards, including making the Long List for the Man Booker Prize in 2017 for her novella *Swallowing*

Mercury. Wioletta chose to leave the Island for Essex in 2016 but it should be remembered how the Isle of Wight played a significant part in her life and how she introduced it first to Polish speakers and now to the world.

Frustratingly little of the Island's home-grown talent, or the talent that has made it their home, has been widely recognised here. It would be great to see a Holsinger Avenue, Khalvati Drive or Krishnamma Park. It would be amazing to be able to say that the High Sheriff of the Isle of Wight is someone like the famous poet Mimi Khalvati or the Man Booker Prize-nominated author Wioletta Grzegorzewska. These women are already great ambassadors for the Island, putting it at the forefront of their literary works and introducing the Island to new audiences; I'm sure they would create some real excitement during their time as ceremonial head of the Island. Or maybe the role of "Isle of Wight Ambassador" needs to be established for talented people like these who wave the flag for the Island out in the wider world.

It is also important to notice how these people all seem to love the Island and have actively incorporated it into their books, their poems, their films or their songs. They seem proud to say they come from here and it would be great to see the Isle of Wight engage more with this side of its identity. In the last census in 2011, 4.6% of people on the Island gave their nationality or ethnic identity as something other than White British or Irish. This might not seem much but actually equates to a figure of almost five hundred more than the entire population of Ventnor.

This segment of the Island's population might not get

much recognition from the local media but it will contain a multitude of interesting characters, successful individuals and remarkable people. Sometimes the Island's lack of diversity is used as a criticism but it's not numbers that matter if we are home to important international and home-grown minority talent and we recognise the contributions of these people which make the Island the place it is. The Island's combination of its unique Isle of Wight traits, its British traits and its international traits together create the most interesting, colourful and vibrant version of itself that the Island can possibly be. If any of these parts are missing then the Island's full story is not being told.

I hope other people have found some of the discoveries we have made about the Island's international history as exciting as I have. It would be great if this book inspires people to look into this side of the Island's history themselves or bring forward their own stories. This is only the start of investigations into this largely unknown but significant aspect of Island life and hopefully it has demonstrated how far this subject can go. There are still many more secrets the Island has to reveal and it could well lead to a *Missing Chapter Part Two*.

Picture Credits

1. Olaudah Equiano. Public Domain, from the British Library via Creative Commons, Licence 1.0.
2. Ira Aldridge. Public Domain, from Biblioteka Narodowa – National Library of Poland via Creative Commons, Licence 1.0.
3. Prince Alemayehu. Courtesy of the National Portrait Gallery.
4. Emperor Haile Selassie. Courtesy of Ventnor and District Local History Society.
5. Maharajah Duleep Singh. Courtesy of the National Portrait Gallery.
6. The Princess of Coorg. Public Domain, from the Slovak National Gallery via Creative Commons.
7. Chang the Giant. Copyright: Wellcome Collection via Creative Commons licence 4.0. Original title: 'Chang Yu-sing the Chinese giant, and Chung Mow, a dwarf. Photograph.'
8. Shinobu Hirota. Courtesy of Carisbrooke Castle Museum.
9. Suri Krishnamma. Courtesy of Suri Krishnamma.

10. Mimi Khalvati. Copyright: Caroline Forbes. Courtesy of Mimi Khalvati.
11. Wioletta Grzegorzewska. Courtesy of Wioletta Grzegorzewska.

Select Bibliography

This list does not include the hundreds of local newspaper articles, birth, marriage, death or census records, directories or first-hand accounts that were used as evidence.

Introduction

Bogle, James & Joanna Bogle. *A Heart for Europe: The Lives of Emperor Charles and Empress Zita of Austria-Hungary* (1990)

Counterpart lease of house and premises called Guadalupe, but formerly called Non Pareil or Sandown Cottage, at Sandown, p. Brading, I.W. (via National Archives)

Craig, F. W. S. *British Parliamentary Election Results: 1885-1918* (1974)

Kilou, Abdenour. Obituary: Mohand Aarav Bessaoud. *The Guardian.* Wednesday 30 January 2002

Lyonga, Nalova (Ed.) *Socrates in Cameroon: The Life and Works of Bernard Nsokika Fonlon* (2010)

Maddy-Weitzman, Bruce. *The Berber Identity Movement and the Challenge to the North African States* (2011)

Soulahian Kuyumijan, Rita. *Archeology of Madness: Komitas, Portrait of an Armenian Icon* (2001)

Black Georgians

Andrews, Kenneth R. *Ships, Money and Politics: Seafaring and Naval Enterprise in the Reign of Charles I* (1991)

Anon. *A Collection of Voyages and Travels*, Vol. 2. (1745)

Costello, Ray. *Black Salt: Seafarers of African Descent on British Ships* (2012)

Duffield, Ian. "The Life and Death of 'Black' John Goff: Aspects of the Black Convict Contribution to Resistance Patterns During the Transportation Era in Eastern Australia", *Australian Journal of Politics and History*, 33.1, April 1987.

Equiano, Olaudah. *The Interesting Narrative of the Life of Olaudah Equiano, Or Gustavus Vassa, the African* (1794)

Extract from the Will of Ellen Robinson (via I.W. Record Office)

Kaufmann, Miranda. *Black Tudors: The Untold Story* (2017)

Kershen, Anne J. (Ed.). *Language, Labour and Migration* (2017)

Killingray, David (Ed.). *Africans in Britain* (2012)

Maclean, Gerald & Nabil Matar. *Britain and the Islamic World, 1558-1713* (2011)

Mountain, Joseph. *Sketches of the Life of Joseph Mountain* (1790)

Olusoga, David. *Black and British* (2016)

Richmond, Legh. *Annals of the Poor* (1815)

The Will of Maria Burns, formerly Inglis (via UCL Legacies of British Slave-Ownership)

Williams, Luke G. *Richmond Unchained: The Biography of the World's First Black Sporting Superstar* (2015)

Black Victorians

Bowers, Keith. *Imperial Exile, Emperor Haile Selassie in Britain 1936-40* (2016)

Boyce Davies, Caroline (Ed.). *Encyclopaedia of the African Diaspora: Origins, Experiences, and Culture*, Vol. 2. (2008)

C.C. (Pseud.). *Anecdotes of Alamayu* (1870)

Dresser, Madge & Andrew Hann. *Slavery and the British Country House* (2013)

Fremmer, Ray. "Henry Sewell... heir to an Empire, demolished a fortune", *The Sunday Gleaner Magazine* (Jamaica Gleaner) 17 August 1980.

Green, Jeffrey. *Samuel Coleridge-Taylor, a Musical Life* (2015)

Greenspan, Ezra. *William Wells Brown: An African American Life* (2014)

Johnson, Thomas L. *Twenty-Eight Years a Slave, or the Story of My Life in Three Continents* (1909)

Ketner, Joseph D. *The Emergence of the African-American Artist: Robert S. Duncanson 1821-1872* (1994)

Killingray, David (Ed.). *Africans in Britain* (2012)

Lindfors, Bernth. *Ira Aldridge: The Last Years 1855-1867* (2011)

Lobb, John (Ed.) *Uncle Tom's Story of His Life: An Autobiography of the Rev. Josiah Henson* (1876)

McCord, Margaret. *The Calling of Katie Makanya* (1997)

Page, Jesse. *Samuel Crowther, The Slave Boy Who Became Bishop of the Niger* (1888)

Profile of Margaret Dunbar – for Ebenezer Robertson (via UCL Legacies of British Slave-Ownership)

Roper, Moses. *Narrative of the Adventures and Escape of Moses Roper from American Slavery* (1848)

Williams, Paul. *Custer and the Sioux, Durnford and the Zulus* (2015)

Indian Residents

Bressey, Caroline. *Empire, Race and the Politics of Anti-caste* (2013)

Dresser, Madge & Andrew Hann. *Slavery and the British Country House* (2013)

Lloyd, James Hendrie (Ed.). *The Philadelphia Medical Journal*, Vol. 8 (1901)

Reeves, Peter. *The Encyclopaedia of the Sri Lankan Diaspora* (2014)

Squibb, Edward Robinson (Ed.). *An Ephemeris of Materia Medica, Pharmacy, Therapeutics and Collateral Information*, Vol. 7 (1903)

Vandal, Pervaiz & Sajida Vandal. *Khalsa College – A Legacy of Bhai Ram Singh* (2007)

Wright, Christopher & Catherine May Gordon. *British and Irish Paintings in Public Collections* (2006)

Indian Visitors

Adams, William Henry Davenport. *Nelson's Hand-book to the Isle of Wight* (1862)

Ahmad, Rafiuddin (Moulvi). "The Queen's Hindustani Diary", *The Strand Magazine*, No. 24, 1892.

Anand, Anita. *Sophia: Princess, Suffragette, Revolutionary* (2015)

Andrews, C. F. *Sadhu Sundar Singh, A Personal Memoir* (1934)

Dutt, Romesh Chunder. *Three Years in Europe, 1868 to 1871* (1896)

Fisher, Michael H. *Counterflows to Colonialism: Indian Travellers and Settlers in Britain 1600-1857* (2006)

Gandhi, M. K. *An Autobiography: The Story of My Experiments with Truth* (2009)

Ilahi, Shereen. *Imperial Violence and the Path to Independence* (2016)

Lal, Mohan. *Travels in the Panjab, Afghanistan & Turkistan, to Balk, Bokhara, and Herat: and A Visit to Great Britain and Germany* (1846)

Lutyens, Mary. *J Krishnamurti: A Life* (2005)

Mogridge, George (Pseud. Old Humphrey). *Owen Gladdon's Wanderings in the Isle of Wight* (1850)

Moore, Lucy. *Maharanis: The Lives and Times of Three Generations of Indian Princesses* (2004)

Risk Allah, Habib (Effendi). *The Thistle and the Cedar of Lebanon* (1854)

Saklatvala, Sehri. *The Fifth Commandment: A Biography of Shapurji Saklatvala* (1991)

Visram, Rozina. *Asians in Britain: 400 Years of History* (2002)

Wadia, Ardaser Sorabjee N. *The Call of the World, Being Reminiscences of a Year's Tour Round the World* (1918)

The Wider World

Alexander, Michael. *Omai, Noble Savage* (1977)

de Beneski, Charles. *A Narrative of the Last Moments of the Life of Don Augustín de Iturbide, Ex-emperor of Mexico* (1825)

Carter, Sarah & Maria Nugent (Eds.) *Mistress of Everything: Queen Victoria in Indigenous Worlds* (2016)

Durrani, Tehmina. *My Feudal Lord* (1995)

im Thurn, Everard F. (Ed.). *Dictionary of National Biography, 1912 Supplement* (1912)

Kanahele, George S. *Emma: Hawaii's Remarkable Queen* (1999)

Lewis, John B. *Darwin's Coral Atoll* (2013)

Lyonga, Nalova (Ed.). *Socrates in Cameroon: The Life and Works of Bernard Nsokika Fonlon* (2010)

McCormick, Eric H. *Omai: Pacific Envoy* (2013)

Milne, John. "Shinobu Hirota", *Nature* (Periodical) 90, 435. 19 December 1912

Peleggi, Maurizio. *Lords of Things: The Fashioning of the Siamese Monarchy's Modern Image* (2002)

Pemba, Tsewang Y. *Young Days in Tibet* (1957)

Saeger, James Schofield. *Francisco Solano López and the Ruination of Paraguay* (2007)

Williams, Mary Wilhelmine. *Dom Pedro the Magnanimous, Second Emperor of Brazil* (2013)

About the Author

James Rayner was born and brought up on the Isle of Wight. His background is in language and literature, which he studied with the University of Iceland and the University of Malmö in Sweden. He has written articles for print and online magazines. This is his first book, which is the culmination of eight months of research.